Study Skills
That Stick

by Dr. Margaret Nuzum

SCHOLASTIC
PROFESSIONAL BOOKS

New York • Toronto • London • Auckland • Sydney
Mexico City • New Delhi • Hong Kong

Cover design by Madalina Stefan
Interior design by Drew Hires
Interior illustrations by Drew Hires

ISBN 0-439-06070-2

Table of Contents

Introduction

Wouldn't it be great if your students learned on their own? It's possible, with your help and guidance, to develop a class of independent, autonomous learners.

To be independent learners, students have to know how to learn as well as what to learn. This book will help you help them.

The first step is to be sure students understand that they must intend to learn, and that you will assist in that process by teaching them not only what but how.

Types of Knowledge

Begin by identifying the types of knowledge that a learner needs:

- **Basic skills:** For each subject there is a set of basic skills that underlie proficiency. These skills, such as math facts, are often learned in isolation and then practiced and combined with other skills.

- **Language skills:** Language is crucial in presenting and comprehending information. For example, students must be able to listen to information in class, follow directions (both oral and written), and extract meaning from the written page.

- **Procedural knowledge:** Students often follow step-by-step instructions to complete a specific task. For example, to solve a long division problem, students must know the sequence of steps needed to get the correct answer.

- **Background knowledge:** Learning is built on foundations which are established through past learning. Make students aware that they can acquire background information through interaction with their environment and other people, as well as through reading, observation, and conversation. Point out that background knowledge is also a foundation on which to build future knowledge.

- **Content knowledge:** In a given subject, students acquire content knowledge. Help students appreciate that knowledge acquired through course work is a foundation for continued growth in that subject area as well as related areas.

- **Strategic knowledge:** The techniques used for learning or achieving a goal are crucial. Acquiring strategies for thinking and learning are skills that students will use for a lifetime.

SPLOME: A Teaching-Learning System

Certain processes guide the acquisition, storage, and use of information. Although these functions are readily apparent in some learners, not all know innately how to approach a task. You can teach students using SPLOME, a system that helps students use what they know and acquire what they need to know. SPLOME stands for

Set goals: Here, a student focuses on the purpose of the task and on the final outcome or product.

Plan: The student organizes a plan to achieve the goal.

Link: The student makes connections, linking information to other subjects or background knowledge.

Organize: The student systematizes the work process.

Monitor: The student monitors progress, with the teacher's help, by revisiting the goal and the plan, and determining the degree of understanding.

Evaluate: The student evaluates the work in relation to the initial purpose.

SPLOME is based on the premise that learning is easier when

- the goal is readily apparent and clearly stated.
- information is organized systematically and set in a framework.
- it is clear why and how information learned in the past supports information learned at the present time.
- a learner uses sets of strategies that facilitate organization, planning, checking, and evaluating.
- a learner has ample time, opportunity, instruction, reinstruction, and practice.
- it occurs over time.

Reflections on Learning

Before reading further, take time to recall your own positive and negative learning experiences. What procedures or strategies did your teachers use to help you complete a learning task? What strategies did you use to complete a learning task? What factors inhibited you from completing a learning task? You might find it helpful to do this with a colleague, sharing your memories and reflections.

When you finish, categorize and prioritize your recollections. If you recall teachers who were nurturing, try to be specific about what they did that made you feel comfortable in the classroom. If a word such as "safe" comes up, it often means that instruction was clear, consistent, or orderly. "Nurturing" may mean that a teacher helped you identify what you knew and coaxed it out of you in a productive way. Educators who recall teachers who did not hand back work or who went too fast rarely recall positive learning experiences. In fact, I have found in the workshops I conduct that teachers who recall positive learning experiences are usually describing teaching practices that closely parallel SPLOME.

Classwork

Your classroom is your laboratory for study skills instruction. It is here that students have the chance to master the essential language and the step-by-step procedures that are a part of your coursework. However, students need to learn how to approach a learning task so they can benefit from your instruction. They need to learn to **S**et goals, **P**lan, **L**ink, **O**rganize, **M**onitor, and **E**valuate their work.

You can teach students to ask questions to find out

- ✔ what they are doing.
- ✔ how they plan to get it done.
- ✔ why they are doing it.
- ✔ what materials they need.
- ✔ whether or not they accomplished the task.
- ✔ what they learned from the work.

When you develop lessons, set your goals with both content and study skills in mind. Here are some tips that I find helpful.

- **Focus your instruction:** Be clear about what is important enough to evaluate.
- **Focus your presentation:** Be clear about how you expect students to learn.
- **Motivate students:** Explain the long-term use of the material on tests and any test-taking policies.
- **Involve students:** Invite them to identify their own expectations and delineate their responsibility for meeting them.
- **Involve parents** so they can understand, and thereby support, your approach.
- **Provide feedback** on how students are learning.
- **Encourage feedback** on how you are teaching.

The best way to prepare students for learning is to model and teach techniques that foster an active, systematic acquisition of knowledge. Strategies on how to focus, pay attention, follow directions, listen, self-question, organize, and plan are not always thought of as study skills, but they are. And you can provide instruction in these while teaching content.

Your Goals

Most school-based direct learning takes place in the classroom so students should be prepared to learn there. Take some time to think about what you believe students should be able to do, or learn to do, in order to benefit from classroom activities. Also, keep in mind what students should learn to do to prepare for independent work.

Lesson Planning

A comprehensive lesson plan is critical to accomplishing multiple objectives. Think of your lessons as analogous to an adventure trip. Establish a lesson planning itinerary. Imagine asking yourself or your students these questions:

1. Where are you going?
2. How will you get there?
3. What will you do along the way?
4. What will you need to bring?

5. How will you organize your time?
6. How will you evaluate the adventure?
7. What are the criteria for success?

Translated into SPLOME, your list would look like this:

Set goals:
- Tell students (or have them describe) what they will learn after you have finished the lesson.
- Let them know what you expect them to do with the topic.

Plan:
- Plan their study activities in class and at home.

Link:
- Link all information so students can see connections between what they learned yesterday and what they will learn today.

Organize:
- Organize your activities logically.
- Provide graphic organizers for students.

Monitor:
- Check to see that students are using activities and any graphic organizers effectively.
- Provide frequent feedback to help students gauge their knowledge and progress.
- Be sure students keep track of their work and your critique of their work.

Evaluate:
- Ask students to assess their achievement and movement toward the goal.

Tip

Call on students to state or paraphrase a lesson's goal. (Then, they can write down this goal on the reproducible on page 16.) You can also call on students to summarize what they have learned at the end of a lesson.

Organization

Organization is a life skill. We all know people who are disorganized and have made it to adulthood. Nevertheless, students will be much better off if they learn to organize their work and materials now.

Remind students of the materials they need for class as well as what the assignment is. Write instructions on the chalkboard in a format such as the one below. Have students copy it on paper to tape to their assignments notebook, binder, or homework book. If students work on computers, send a notice by e-mail. Explain that being organized for classwork is part of a student's grade.

Bring to Class:
For my _____ class I need to bring
1. _____
2. _____
3. _____
The assignment is _____
_____
_____

Discuss and model strategies for students who tend to "forget" things. One effective way to handle this is to hypothetically state a problem one or more students may be having and invite others in the class to tell how they handle the same situation. For example, if a student has trouble remembering to bring materials to class, ask other students what strategies they use to remember.

Repeat the strategies offered and ask students to choose one to try. If a particular student fails to remember books or materials again, use the same approach but this time make it a one-on-one discussion. Have the individual student name a strategy that could help solve this problem.

Class Participation

Students must also learn to monitor their own behavior and learning in class. To benefit the most from class discussions and other activities, students must learn to

✔ **stay focused and on task.**

✔ **listen effectively, so that they**
  • know when something important is happening.
  • know who is talking.
  • know the main point and important details.
  • can paraphrase oral discussion.
  • know what to remember and learn.

✔ **participate in class discussion, being able to**
  • anticipate and prepare.
  • speak up.

✔ **follow directions, both oral and written.**

✔ **develop and practice note-taking skills.**

✔ **write down assignments.**

✔ **recall what they have learned.**

Essentially, students must be good listeners with the capacity to pay attention, follow directions, and remember what the teacher and their classmates have said. On the flip side, participation in discussions gives students a way to show what they know and to

test the clarity and degree of understanding of their ideas. Raising questions is the way students learn to identify what they don't understand and what they still need to learn. If necessary, model questioning for students.

For students who have difficulty staying focused and tend to miss directions or critical instruction, try the "Dot System." Tell each of these students privately that together you will develop a special system to help keep the student on track. Once in agreement, when the student goes off task, put a gummed dot, for instance, next to the place in a book or written assignment where the student digressed. The dot serves as a reminder to the student to get back on track. If you also keep track of this in your record book, after awhile, you will be able to identify patterns of off-task behaviors. Sometimes students are really lost, and at other times their attention has simply wandered from the task. Keep the dot sheets on your desk. Sometimes merely moving toward them or lifting them from your desk will refocus students.

Discussion

To get the most out of their time spent in class, students must know what is going on. They must be good listeners, capable of understanding a question and responding on target. As a teacher, you will want to help students prepare to participate in class discussions. What skills must students have to be effective? Share these criteria with the class:

✔ *A good listener*
  - is attentive.
  - understands the form of a conversation.
  - knows the main idea.
  - can summarize.
  - links information to reading.

✔ *A responsive student*
  - understands the question.
  - has a foundation of related knowledge.
  - has acquired information from discussion, reading, or the lesson.
  - has the ability to tie information together.
  - has the ability to find words to express an idea.

Share the following goals with students to help them become better class discussion participants:

✔ Know the topic under discussion, and the purpose for discussing it.

✔ Identify some questions to answer.

✔ Know when to speak.

✔ Note how other material fits into the discussion.

✔ Be aware of who is talking and the speaker's style.

As you know, students have different strengths, and this becomes very evident in class discussions. Some students are talkative or inquisitive, and others are shy or unsure of themselves. To keep a discussion from being dominated by talkative students and to draw less vocal ones into the discussion, try this: State a non-participating student's name, pause, then pose a question. This gives the student advance notice that he or she is expected to respond; it also signifies that this question is especially for that student.

Tip
If students have difficulty expressing themselves during a discussion, give them a bit of time and then if necessary, provide a choice of responses. Often, this enables students to give an answer and perhaps elaborate on it. If the student is still having problems, move on to another who can build on the answer. This approach remains supportive while keeping the discussion moving.

Taking Notes

Teach students to take notes so that they have a clear record of a class discussion and can remember the points that were emphasized. Learning to take notes is a developmental process and not all students will find the same techniques helpful, so it is important to provide alternatives. The most supportive activity in the instructional process is to provide students with a partially completed, ready-made, fill-in-the-blank outline, such as the reproducible found on page 17.

Note-taking is particularly difficult during a rousing class discussion about a novel or current event. Opinions are expressed, clarified, and revised. Digression is likely. Although

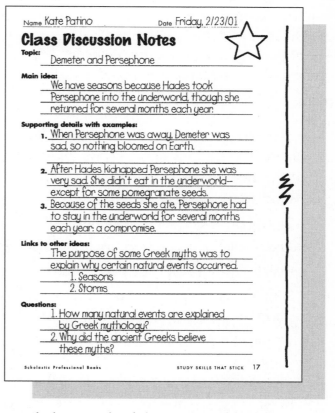

Name Kate Patino   Date Friday, 2/23/01

Class Discussion Notes

Topic:
Demeter and Persephone

Main idea:
We have seasons because Hades took Persephone into the underworld, though she returned for several months each year.

Supporting details with examples:
1. When Persephone was away, Demeter was sad, so nothing bloomed on Earth.

2. After Hades kidnapped Persephone she was very sad. She didn't eat in the underworld— except for some pomegranate seeds.
3. Because of the seeds she ate, Persephone had to stay in the underworld for several months each year: a compromise.

Links to other ideas:
The purpose of some Greek myths was to explain why certain natural events occurred.
    1. Seasons
    2. Storms

Questions:
    1. How many natural events are explained by Greek mythology?
    2. Why did the ancient Greeks believe these myths?

Scholastic Professional Books   STUDY SKILLS THAT STICK   17

discussions are stimulating, students can easily lose track of the point and be left confused or with incorrect assumptions. You can help by summarizing the points of the discussion that you want to emphasize. Be sure to provide time for students to jot down these points. If you have students copy notes from the board, discuss what is on the board after, not during, their copying exercise. (Some students may have difficulty copying. Be sure to consider alternatives for them.)

You can also structure lessons and discussions so that they are orderly—with a clear topic, main points, and a logical progression. Tell students when an item is important.

Model and guide note clarification. Direct questions to help students organize, focus, and elaborate.

Despite these efforts, many students cannot listen well or participate if they are required to take notes. Give students time near the end of class to work with a partner or to independently review and revise their class notes. Have students use the reproducible on page 18 as a guide. This activity can also be done as homework.

With practice you can help students learn good note-taking strategies by modeling the following steps, on chart paper or a chalkboard, during a class discussion:

- Date the notes.
- Write the related chapter, text pages, or relevant outside reading in the margin next to the notes. (Try using a different-colored marker or chalk.)
- Identify the topic or aim of the class lesson, discussion, or activity. Write it at the top of the notes.
- Clarify the subtopics or main ideas discussed in the class.
- Add, circle, or star any information that supports the topic and any subtopics.
- Develop a personal code that helps coordinate related ideas.
- Put a check next to any information that is confusing or incomplete. Then clarify this information by reading the text or asking someone who can help.
- Jot down some questions that might show up on a test.

Class notes are a student's link to the content. Moreover, they provide a key to what you think is important. Good notes serve to clarify reading, focus preparation for class discussion, and help with reviewing and studying for tests. They organize and integrate material, providing a way for students to check their own understanding of the topic.

Tip
Remind students to use their paraphrasing skills when taking notes, especially when using the information for a written report.

Following Directions
"What?" "I don't know what to do."

Strengthening direction-following skills is a worthwhile ongoing objective for students of all ages. The ultimate goal is to have students learn to monitor their behavior and to curb any tendencies to act impulsively, with inaccurate information, without a time frame, or without clear expectations.

Help students learn self-monitoring strategies that will enable them to get important (and accurate) information. Students need to be able to

- ✔ identify when they are not paying attention.
- ✔ restate directions to themselves (or paraphrase them orally to the teacher) before they begin work.
- ✔ identify the purpose, expectation, and time-frame for an assignment.
- ✔ ask questions for clarification.

Begin by developing the value of knowing what you, as the teacher, expect. Be sure that students know that learning to follow directions has consequences far beyond the classroom.

When you give instruction, model the behavior you expect of them. Show students how to check their own understanding by paraphrasing the commands aloud. Encourage them to ask guiding questions that define the task. For example:

- ✔ What am I supposed to do?
- ✔ What is the purpose?
- ✔ How much time do I have?
- ✔ When should I do this?

Provide guided practice. Ask students the same questions that you have modeled. For example:

- ✔ What are you supposed to do?
- ✔ Why are you doing this?
- ✔ How long will it take?

Set parameters. Don't let students start until they can paraphrase the directions. If they can't because they don't understand them, encourage students to ask for help. Help students identify what is unclear and how to express their confusion. Provide ongoing practice on a daily basis as necessary.

Setting Goals

Put this form in your binder and fill it out during or immediately after class. Every day, write down the learning goal for each class.

Monday   / /

Science	
English/Language Arts	
History/Social Studies	
Mathematics	

Tuesday   / /

Science	
English/Language Arts	
History/Social Studies	
Mathematics	

Wednesday   / /

Science	
English/Language Arts	
History/Social Studies	
Mathematics	

Thursday   / /

Science	
English/Language Arts	
History/Social Studies	
Mathematics	

Friday   / /

Science	
English/Language Arts	
History/Social Studies	
Mathematics	

Class Discussion Notes

Topic:

_____

Main idea:

_____

_____

_____

Supporting details with examples:

1. _____

_____

_____

2. _____

_____

_____

3. _____

_____

_____

Links to other ideas:

_____

_____

_____

Questions:

_____

_____

_____

Updating Class Notes

Take five minutes each day to review and revise your class notes. Once you have completed each step on this chart, check it off.

Have I...	English	History	Science	Math
dated my notes?				
indicated related chapters/text pages?				
identified main topic of lesson?				
clarified main idea of lesson?				
added supporting details?				
added examples?				
linked related information?				
added topic headings, numbers, and bullets to organize the material?				
addressed confusing or incomplete information?				
written down possible test topics or questions?				

Reading

"The teacher said to read it, not to learn it."

Non-fiction

Students often take things literally. For many students, reading means scanning the words, passing over the text. These students fail to understand or remember the content either because they don't know all the skills involved in reading, or they don't know how to read to learn. You can help.

Be sure students have a solid foundation in the knowledge essential to reading:

Basic skills: phonics, word-attack skills, sight words, pacing

Language skills: appropriate development of
- general vocabulary
- content specific vocabulary
- knowledge of sentence structure
- knowledge of paragraph structure

Procedural knowledge: process, procedure, or order used to
- decode words
- organize and use the structure of language

Background knowledge: relevant information that forms the foundation for integration of new knowledge

Strategic knowledge: routines and techniques to organize and monitor learning such as
- previewing
- outlining
- self-questioning

Many students have insight into their own reading skills and what they know about reading. Others are not certain about what they know, but they are candid about how they see themselves as readers, and they can identify what confuses them. Have students fill out the Reading Profile on page 27 and the Reading Skills Profile on page 28 to help you understand their reading habits and skills.

Using SPLOME for Reading

You can help students become active, engaged, resourceful readers and also develop their reading skills with SPLOME. Model the following tasks for students to target. Distribute the reproducible on page 29 for students to use when completing reading assignments.

<u>S</u>et goals:

Help your students focus on the shared goal by
- identifying the purpose of the reading.
- identifying the scope of the reading.
- letting them know how the content will be used.

<u>P</u>lan:

With your students, practice
- previewing the chapter and its questions found at the end.
- predicting results or information.
- selecting unfamiliar terms and vocabulary.
- planning and allocating time.

<u>L</u>ink:

Help students to realize how the current reading assignment builds on or is interconnected with past reading.

<u>O</u>rganize:

Help students organize by
- letting them know what materials they need.
- suggesting that they outline the chapter.

<u>M</u>onitor:

Suggest that students check for understanding by
- self-questioning.
- reviewing their outlines.
- summarizing the chapter.
- writing definitions to terms and vocabulary in their own words.
- identifying confusing material and raising questions.
- rereading as necessary.

<u>E</u>valuate:

Remind students to ask themselves:
- Did I learn the terms?
- Can I state the main point?
- Am I prepared to talk about it?
- Does my work show what I know?
- Can I apply my knowledge?

Language Skills

The foundation for reading comprehension is the structure of language. Students need to understand vocabulary and how it is used in written sentences. The first line of attack in comprehension is improving vocabulary and knowledge of important terms. You can help students by

- surveying material to identify any difficult words and important terminology.
- providing the definitions before students read a passage.

Ask students to note any unfamiliar words they encounter while reading at home. Suggest that they write the word on a post-it and use it to mark the place in the book. They can then find the meanings of all the unfamiliar words after reading by asking the teacher or classmates, or by looking up the word in a dictionary. Encourage students to reread the sentence or passage with the word's meaning fresh in their minds. Suggest that students also write the word meanings on the post-its and keep the post-its in place. Chances are they may need help with the word again when reviewing the text for a test.

Tip
Have students keep word journals or set aside sections of their writing journals for new vocabulary words. Students might also enjoy using a rolodex to keep track of new words. Encourage students to revisit these words once a week and to use them in their writing.

To improve general vocabulary, set up a flexible weekly plan. Select words that are relevant to a subject students are studying. Provide students with the reproducible on page 30. Have them write the words in the left column and the definitions in the right column. Explain that students can fold back the page so only the words are visible. They can then work with a classmate or someone at home to review and master the new words. Note that you can provide extra copies of the reproducible page for students to use at home when doing assignments.

Paragraphs

Students need a framework for reading. It is therefore essential to help them understand the structure, order, and organization of a paragraph. When students know the structure of a paragraph and what type of information is included, they can read more efficiently and effectively and respond logically. Teach students that a paragraph is

- ✔ unified.
- ✔ coherent.
- ✔ logical.
- ✔ directed.

Also, let students know that the paragraph structure includes

- ✔ one topic.
- ✔ a main idea.
- ✔ interrelated sentences that support and develop the main idea.
- ✔ a concluding sentence that summarizes or moves the topic forward.

Of course, students need to know that the main idea is not always in the first sentence, but can also be found at the end, sometimes in the middle, and is occasionally only inferred.

To read a paragraph with understanding, students should be able to

- ✔ understand the structure of a paragraph.
- ✔ identify the topic of a paragraph.
- ✔ find the main idea sentence in a paragraph.
- ✔ paraphrase the main idea sentence.
- ✔ identify the related details in a paragraph.
- ✔ identify whether the details are facts, examples, descriptions, opinions, and so forth.
- ✔ outline a well-constructed paragraph.

Knowing the structure of paragraphs enables students to develop procedural knowledge skills so they can remember what they have read and how it is related. Recalling one main idea and then connecting the relevant details, like a branch to a tree trunk, is easier than recalling a series of unrelated facts.

Using the reproducible form on page 31, help students review paragraph structure. Choose a well-constructed paragraph for students to read, or use the one provided below. Note that this activity also gives students practice in paraphrasing. You may wish to have students work in small groups until they are comfortable with the exercise and with paragraph skills.

> The opening of the Berlin Wall in November 1989 symbolized the end of the Cold War. This 110-mile-long wall had been built by Communist East Germany in 1961 to keep its citizens from fleeing to the West. Up until then, large numbers of East Germans had fled to the West. Many people still tried to escape, and some made it, but more than 170 others lost their lives in the attempt. In 1989, popular protests against travel and emigration restrictions forced the East German government to open the wall. By the end of the next year, East Germany and West Germany had joined to become the non-Communist country of Germany.

Active Reading

Students must be aware that the purpose of reading textbooks is to learn some specified content. Unfortunately, learning is not always the goal for some students.

For example, I was reading with Sam, an enthusiastic student who sped through the material barely catching his breath.

"What is your purpose in reading this material?" I asked.

"To get to the end," he responded.

"Oh," I said, "then why am I here?"

Without skipping a beat, he looked at me and said, "To help me get to the end faster."

Sam was clear about his purpose for reading: To get through it! However, readers like Sam are not happy or productive readers. They are not active readers. To read actively, students must know how to

✔ discern the structure and organization of a paragraph.

✔ identify the main idea.

✔ know relevant facts, reasons, and examples that develop the main idea.

✔ identify new vocabulary and relevant terminology.

✔ paraphrase a sentence to reduce it to the essential targeted meaning.

✔ outline and identify information that is confusing.

Help students become active readers by modeling the teaching strategies that follow. You can also have students complete the Reading Checklist found on page 33 while they are mastering these strategies.

Preview and link.
- Discuss the upcoming chapter or topic and how it ties into past and future learning.
- Have students preview the chapter or next assignment and list what they will learn.
- Guide students in identifying vocabulary words.

Develop organizing and learning techniques.
- Use the chapter format—title and subtitles—as an outline and have students fill in important details.
- Have students develop their own outline.
- Have students develop questions about what they read.

Evaluate quality of reading.
- Have students review questions they developed, along with any answers, in class or in groups.
- Help students answer unanswered questions.
- Encourage class discussions.

Textbook Reading

Here is a plan to help students read a textbook effectively.

Before Reading

Preview a chapter: Have students read the bold and italicized parts of the chapter to develop an organizing framework for the content. Spend a few minutes in class discussion previewing the text content. The preview helps students know what is important to look for in the chapter. (See page 32 for a reproducible that students can use for previewing.)

Outline a chapter: Good outlining skills help students focus information in an orderly way. Teach students to pinpoint the main idea of each section and list the facts, reasons, and examples that support and develop that idea. Often, students can use the heads and subheads of a textbook chapter as the basis for an outline. While students are learning this skill, have them compare their outlines in groups. Suggest that students keep their chapter outlines in a specified place in their notebooks for future reference.

During Reading

Select important terms: Selecting and defining important terms as they read enables students to set up a self-testing system for future test preparation.

Questions: When students develop questions about the content of the chapter—short answer, multiple choice, and essay—they gain another opportunity to figure out what is important. Use their questions in game settings, for homework, or even on a test.

After Reading

Answering written questions: Both teacher-developed and student-created questions provide opportunities to answer written questions. Students can practice answering different kinds of questions in class to develop writing skills. Use the short answer or essay questions that students create and have individual students answer the questions. Students can also work with a partner to compare answers and develop better ones. Write a composite group answer to model the development of sound test answers. Collect and evaluate students' in-class writing.

> **Tip**
> Enlist the support of parents in your program for teaching active reading. Explain your goals and let them know what you are doing in class. Suggest ways they can help their child achieve these goals.

Chapter Outline

On the chalkboard, draw the following chart and model the chapter outlining process for your students with a chapter you choose. Explain to students how to use the chart when outlining a chapter, using these directions:

1. On the top of the page, write the subject, chapter title, and pages.

2. In the left column, write the subtopic as given in the chapter.

3. In the right column, write relevant information that supports and develops the subtopic.

4. Then, in the left column, write a question about the material that will help you study.

5. Use a three-hole punch and put the page in a binder or separate notebook. Use the outline to help you study.

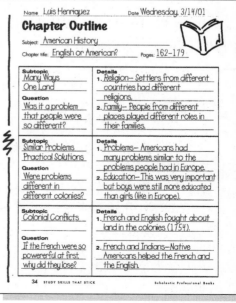

Name Luis Henriquez   Date Wednesday, 3/14/01

Chapter Outline

Subject: American History

Chapter title: English or American?   Pages: 162–179

Subtopic / Question	Details
Subtopic Many Ways One Land **Question** Was it a problem that people were so different?	1. Religion— Settlers from different countries had different religions. 2. Family— People from different places played different roles in their families.
Subtopic Similar Problems Practical Solutions **Question** Were problems different in different colonies?	1. Problems— Americans had many problems similar to the problems people had in Europe. 2. Education—This was very important but boys were still more educated than girls (like in Europe).
Subtopic Colonial Conflicts **Question** If the French were so powerful at first, why did they lose?	1. French and English fought about land in the colonies (1754). 2. French and Indians—Native Americans helped the French and the English.

34   STUDY SKILLS THAT STICK   Scholastic Professional Books

Then, provide students with the reproducible on page 34 to help them create their own chapter outlines. If students run out of reproducible chapter outline forms while studying at home, they can make their own by folding a piece of paper into thirds and using the left third of the paper for the subtopics and questions, and the right two-thirds of the paper for the relevant supporting information.

Fiction

Students also need to know how to use active reading for fiction. Although fiction differs from expository writing, students can still apply many of the same skills. For example, they can set goals by making predictions. This not only provides a purpose for reading but also a focus for monitoring progress. It can also motivate students to continue reading to see if their predictions come true.

Use the reproducibles on pages 35–37 to help students identify the framework (plot sequence) of a story and to monitor the changes in characters as they develop.

Familiarize students with the types of questions generally asked about fiction. You'll find these listed on page 77 in the Test Preparation section.

Encourage independent reading at home in addition to the books students read as part of their classwork. Be available to help your students select a book, but also teach them to use the following strategies when selecting a book on their own for independent reading:

- ✔ Survey the book cover and read the title. Does the book appeal to you?
- ✔ Identify the author. Have you read any other books by this author?
- ✔ Read the blurb on the back of the book or on the jacket cover to learn more about the story.
- ✔ Be sure the book is not too easy or too difficult.
- ✔ Read a few pages of the book to see if it interests you.
- ✔ Scan any illustrations to learn more about the story.
- ✔ Ask friends if they have read the book. Would they recommend it?

Tip
Enlist parents or other family members in helping students enjoy independent reading. Send home a list of tips such as the following:
- Seek recommendations from the local librarian, other parents, bookstore clerks, or book reviews.
- Keep an ongoing list of potential books and authors.
- Allow enough time to browse when visiting a library or bookstore.
- Read some of the books your child reads so you can talk about them together.

Name _____   Date _____

Reading Profile

Think about the statements below and put a check in the box that best describes how you feel. Then, complete the sentences at the bottom of the page.

Statement	Yes	No
1. I like to read.		
2. Reading is hard for me.		
3. I like a family member to help me read.		
4. I like to read alone.		
5. I like to read aloud.		
6. I like to read silently.		
7. I like to read books that are easy.		
8. I often pick books that seem too hard.		
9. I like to read books that are challenging.		
10. I often do not finish books.		
11. I always have a book to read.		
12. I prefer to pick my own books.		
13. I prefer to get my books from my teacher.		
14. I prefer to get my books from school.		
15. I prefer to get my books from the library.		
16. I prefer to get my books from home.		

★ My favorite type of book is _____.

★ My favorite book is _____.

★ My favorite author is _____.

★ If I could change something about the way I read, I would like to _____

_____

Name _____   Date _____

Reading Skills Profile

Think about the statements below and put a check in the box that best describes what you do. As you think of them, add more details about your reading skills.

Statement	Yes	No
1. I can sound out words.		
2. I can divide words into syllables.		
3. I know when I don't understand a word.		
4. I ask for help when I don't know a word.		
5. I guess the meaning when I don't know a word.		
6. I understand what I read.		
7. I daydream when reading.		
8. I lose my place often.		
9. I can identify the main idea.		
10. I can identify details.		
11. I recognize facts.		
12. I recognize opinions.		
13. I can interpret what I read.		
14. I remember what I read.		

★ _____

★ _____

★ _____

Scholastic Professional Books

Name _____   Date _____

Using SPLOME for Reading

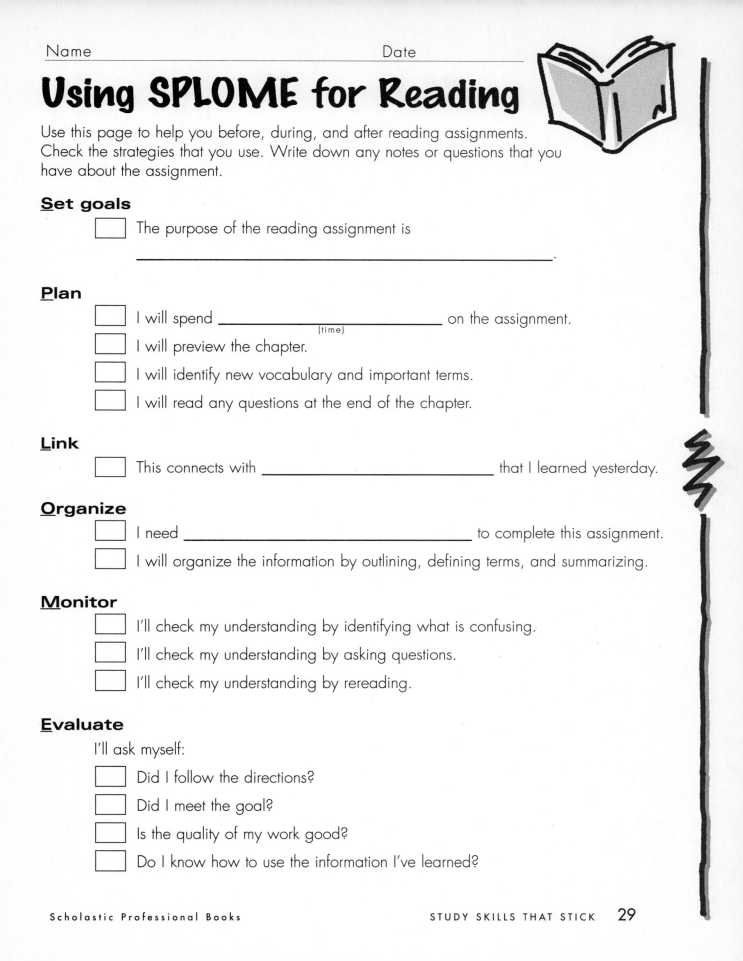

Use this page to help you before, during, and after reading assignments.
Check the strategies that you use. Write down any notes or questions that you
have about the assignment.

Set goals

☐ The purpose of the reading assignment is

_____.

Plan

☐ I will spend _____ on the assignment.

(time)

☐ I will preview the chapter.

☐ I will identify new vocabulary and important terms.

☐ I will read any questions at the end of the chapter.

Link

☐ This connects with _____ that I learned yesterday.

Organize

☐ I need _____ to complete this assignment.

☐ I will organize the information by outlining, defining terms, and summarizing.

Monitor

☐ I'll check my understanding by identifying what is confusing.

☐ I'll check my understanding by asking questions.

☐ I'll check my understanding by rereading.

Evaluate

I'll ask myself:

☐ Did I follow the directions?

☐ Did I meet the goal?

☐ Is the quality of my work good?

☐ Do I know how to use the information I've learned?

Vocabulary List

Use the chart below to list any unfamiliar words that come up in your reading. Provide a definition for each word. Study the words and their meanings. When you are ready, fold back the page at the line between the words and definitions. Then, read the words and see if you remember the definitions.

Subject: _____ Chapter: _____

WORD	DEFINITION

Paragraph Outline

1. Read the assigned paragraph.

2. Write, in your own words,
- the topic.
- the main idea.
- relevant details and examples that explain, elaborate, or support the main idea.
- a conclusion.

Topic: _____

Main idea (paraphrase): _____

_____

Details and examples: 1. _____

_____

2. _____

_____

3. _____

_____

4. _____

_____

Conclusion: _____

_____

_____

_____

3. Retell the passage to a partner using the outline that you made above.

4. On another sheet of paper, rewrite the paragraph using the outline that you made. Compare your written paragraph to the one that you read.

Chapter Preview

Main Topic:

_____

Things I'll learn about:

- _____

- _____

- _____

- _____

- _____

Words I'll need to learn:

- _____   - _____

- _____   - _____

- _____   - _____

- _____   - _____

- _____   - _____

Questions I have about the topic:

- _____

- _____

- _____

- _____

Reading Checklist

Check off the following steps as you complete each one.

A. *Before you start reading, preview the chapter. This will help focus your reading.*

_____ 1. Read the title. What does it mean? What is the topic of the chapter?

_____ 2. Link the topic to the previous chapters and to what you already know.

_____ 3. Read the introduction and all of the headings.

_____ 4. Study any pictures, drawings, graphs, and charts. Read the captions.

_____ 5. Identify important or new terms.

_____ 6. Read the summary and the questions at the end of the chapter.

_____ 7. Figure out the purpose of this chapter and what you will learn.

B. *While you're reading, remember to follow these steps:*

_____ 1. Read the heading of the first section again. Then read the rest of the section.

_____ 2. Note the main idea sentence and paraphrase it.

_____ 3. Note the details and examples that support the main idea.

_____ 4. Reread the paragraph if you cannot state the main idea.

_____ 5. Jot notes and the corresponding page numbers on post-its, index cards, or a desig-
nated sheet in your notebook to help you remember important information in the text.

_____ 6. Repeat steps 1–5 above as you come to each new section.

_____ 7. Outline the chapter as you go.

C. *After reading, the next steps can help you understand and remember what
you have read.*

_____ 1. Summarize the chapter.

_____ 2. Link this information to previous chapters, lessons, and other reading.

_____ 3. List the important terms and define them.

_____ 4. Note any confusing information so you can ask your teacher or classmates.

_____ 5. Write three questions about this chapter.

_____ 6. Write down any possible test questions.

Chapter Outline

Subject: _____

Chapter title: _____   Pages: _____

Subtopic _____ _____ **Question** _____ _____ _____	**Details** 1._____ _____ _____ 2._____ _____ _____
Subtopic _____ _____ **Question** _____ _____ _____	**Details** 1._____ _____ _____ 2._____ _____ _____
Subtopic _____ _____ **Question** _____ _____ _____	**Details** 1._____ _____ _____ 2._____ _____ _____

Scholastic Professional Books

Name _____ Date _____

Predicting

Book Title: _____

Author: _____

_____

Chapter Title or Number: _____

Prediction: _____

_____

Actual: _____

_____

_____

Chapter Title or Number: _____

Prediction: _____

_____

Actual: _____

_____

_____

Chapter Title or Number: _____

Prediction: _____

_____

Actual: _____

_____

Chapter Record—Fiction

Book Title: _____

Author: _____

Chapter title or number: _____

Main idea of the chapter: _____

_____

_____

Character	Description/Purpose
1.	
2.	
3.	
4.	

Plot sequence:

1. _____

2. _____

3. _____

4. _____

Important changes:

1. _____

2. _____

3. _____

4. _____

Scholastic Professional Books

Name _____ Date _____

Story Summary

Fill in the organizer below to help you summarize the story.
Add extra boxes as needed.

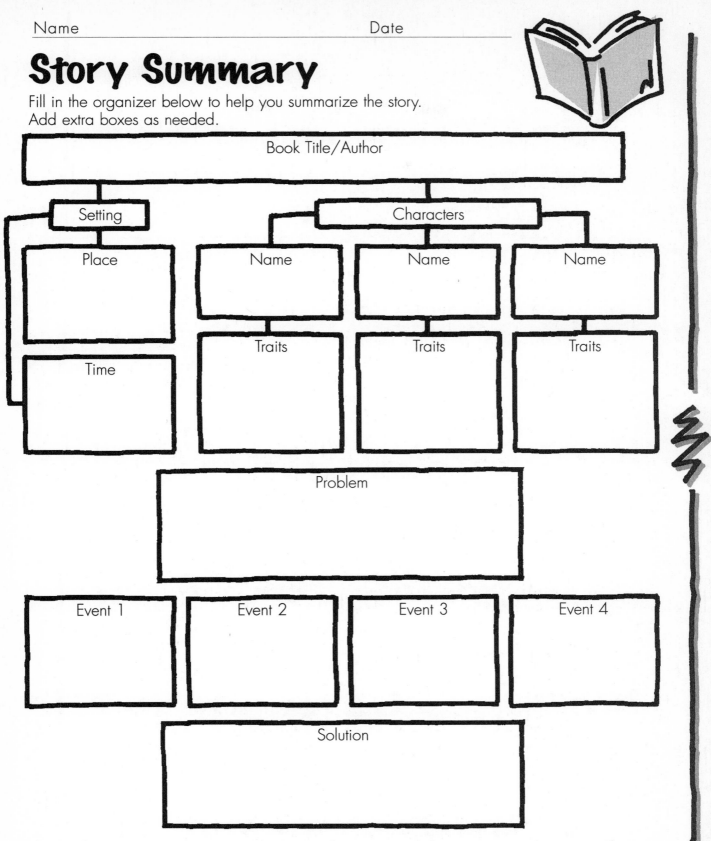

Book Title/Author

Setting

Characters

Place

Name

Name

Name

Time

Traits

Traits

Traits

Problem

Event 1

Event 2

Event 3

Event 4

Solution

Using the information above, write a paragraph summarizing the story on another piece of paper.

Writing

As you emphasize vocabulary, sentence comprehension, and paragraph structure in reading, you can help students apply these concepts to their written work. In other words, use the texts and fiction that students read as models for different types of writing.

Most students need guided instruction in writing. You are no doubt familiar with these students:

- Kris, who says over and over, "I can't think what to write about."
- Jenna, who immediately throws herself into a writing assignment but doesn't complete it.
- Jorge, whose project seems to contain several themes.

Students like Kris tend to get stuck when told to write about anything they like. The assignment is too open-ended, and they have trouble developing a plan. They have too many ideas and spend an enormous amount of mental energy self-censoring, trying to select, and trying to arrange. Students like Jenna, who fail to take the time to think before writing, don't develop a plan that they can carry out. Students like Jorge don't know how to pare down their ideas or recognize those that are unrelated.

For all of these students a systematic writing plan will help. Just as students benefit from direct instruction in systematic reading skills, they need instruction in writing.

Tip

Set up a corner in the classroom with writing materials. Encourage students to use your writing corner as a model and set up a similar place at home. Things to include: assignments, relevant textbooks, a dictionary and thesaurus, proofreading and editing checklists, copies of blank forms, paper, pencils, and a computer and printer.

Using SPLOME for Writing

Both you and your students can use SPLOME for writing
assignments. As the teacher, you can do the following:

Set goals:

- Tell students the purpose of the assignment
  and the type of writing required. Discuss
  what the writing is supposed to accomplish
  and how it will be used.

Plan:

- Help students plan by providing a time frame, as well as a system for
  selecting a topic, and getting and organizing information.

Link:

- Encourage students to relate the task to a previous experience, which depending
  on the assignment, might include connecting to class lessons or personal experience. Have students summarize the knowledge that they need to complete the
  assignment.

Organize:

- Remind students to have all necessary materials within reach before they
  begin to write.

Monitor:

- Work with students to check their progress. Have students refer to the
  original assignment to ensure that they are on track. Remind them to use
  their paragraph checklist.

Evaluate

- Invite students to make their own assessment. This gives them a better feeling
  of ownership of a written piece. At a later time you can make your own
  assessment and sit with each student to compare the evaluations.

You can also give students their own set of SPLOME reminders to use when doing
writing assignments. Provide copies of the reproducible found on page 45.

Developing a Paragraph

Write a question or writing assignment on the chalkboard. You can use the question
provided below, or feel free to use one of your own. Teach students to write a coherent
paragraph by modeling the following procedure:

> What was the pony express and why was it important?

1. Read the question carefully and think about what it really means.
2. State the question in your own words.
3. Brainstorm: List all possible ideas or details related to the topic.
4. Write a possible main idea sentence.
5. Check to see if each detail on your list supports or develops the main idea. Eliminate or replace details that don't.
6. Put a descriptive word and an example next to each detail.
7. Group details that are related and can be included in one sentence.
8. Number groups of details in logical order for the paragraph.
9. Rewrite the topic sentence and develop it fully.
10. Write supporting sentences using the details. (Say the sentences before writing them.)
11. Read the paragraph.
12. Write a concluding sentence that summarizes or moves the paragraph on to the next one.
13. Reread, revise, and edit your paragraph.
14. Proofread your work.

Provide students with the reproducibles on pages 46–48. Suggest that they keep these in their notebooks (or somewhere handy) to consult when they have a writing assignment.

Writing Stories

When writing a story, students need to introduce characters, monitor their progress or changes, and focus on the plot sequence. One way to help students accomplish this is by incorporating some of these details into the brainstorming process. Copy the charts below onto the chalkboard to use while working with students as a group to develop some characters or settings in class. Later, students can use these characters and settings in their own stories.

Characters

Name	Description	Problem	Purpose in story

Setting

Place	Time	Description	Purpose in story

Next, provide students with the reproducible on page 48 to use while they are plotting out a story. Ask them to select a character and setting from the list on the chalkboard to use in their own plots.

Responding to Books

By keeping a journal in which they respond to the books they have read, students not only focus on what they read, but they also develop useful material for writing book reports, reviews, and original stories. Provide students with a copy of the reproducible found on page 49. It is filled with questions that prompt them to think and write about the books they read in a meaningful way. Another fun way for students to connect to what they read is a creative writing activity where they "carry on a dialogue" with a character based on one of their favorite quotes from a book. They can keep track of these quotes using the reproducible on page 51. For more traditional book reports, you can find a helpful outline on page 50.

Writing Research Reports

"I can get it done."
"It won't take much time."
"It's only a draft."

Many students have trouble getting started on a research project because they don't know where to start or how to proceed. Research papers present students with a number of tasks that require them to identify the topic, organize material from several sources, use a particular format, and manage their time. You can use the research report as a means to teach skills and strategies for completing any project effectively.

Let students know the following steps to writing a successful research report.

✔ **Define the scope:**
  • Help students understand the specifics of the assignment.
  • Give a due date.
  • Define the purpose of the report.
  • List the components of the report.
  • Provide them with a written outline, if needed.

✔ **Use a calendar:**
  • On a monthly wall calendar, mark the start and end date of the project to remind students how much time they have.

- Then, mark each of the mini due dates along the way. This will help the students understand that they must finish certain tasks before moving on to the next.
- You can pass out the reproducible calendar found on page 52 for students to use.

✔ **Select a topic:**
- Help students pick a manageable topic: broad enough to find material and narrow enough to be interesting.

✔ **Gather resources:**
- Arrange for students to go to the school or public library to gather books, articles, materials from Web sites, and any other helpful resources.
- Make sure that there is sufficient information on the topic to meet the needs of the report.

✔ **Develop an initial outline:**
- Help students develop a broad outline of the paper by examining research materials and then brainstorming.

✔ **Take notes:**
- Model how students can use their outlines to help structure their notes by writing each topic and subtopic at the top of a piece of paper or index card.
- Suggest that students write on only one side of the paper and explain that the notes are easier to read if students leave a space between each line.
- Remind students to paraphrase the information they read and write their notes under the appropriate subtopic.

✔ **Create a bibliography:**
- Suggest that students keep track of bibliographical information for each reference on a note card or in the margin of their notes.

✔ **Write a first draft:**
- Have students read through their notes and number the information in the sequence needed for the report. (Some students like to cut up their notes and tape them onto another sheet of paper in the appropriate order.)
- Point out that students do not have to write the first draft all at once. For some students it is less burdensome to alternate between note-taking and writing.

✔ **Revise:**
- Pair students to assist one another with revisions.
- Have students note and address unanswered questions or gaps in information, paragraph structure, transitions that need more work, and the clarity of the opening and closing statements.

✔ **Write a final draft:**
- Have students use the suggested revisions in their final draft.
- Point out that it may take more than one attempt to achieve a final draft that meets a writer's goals.

✔ **Proofread:**
- Remind students that presentation is very important.
- Have them use their proofreading checklists to make their papers as error-free as possible.

Editing and Proofreading

Often students' written work is off target due to organizational problems. Sometimes students do not outline before they start to write; or if there is an outline, they do not follow it. If poor organization is apparent after a student has submitted a draft, try the following idea: Ask the student to outline the work just as he or she would outline a text. Then, have the student identify the main idea of each paragraph and list the details that support it. You can model the process and then have the student complete the exercise in the classroom. To practice the process, have pairs of student exchange papers, or perhaps work on a paper from another class. Depending on the class culture, you might also examine students' work as a group exercise. However, be careful not to embarrass students who do not want to share their writing.

Outlining afterward is like placing an exoskeleton on a body of work. It provides a shape and form for the work. Once the shape becomes obvious to students, they can reformat their existing work.

For fiction, students might ask themselves questions such as:

✔ Do the characters have life? Are they believable?
✔ Is the setting realistic in relation to the problem?
✔ Do the characters or settings need more description?
✔ Is there a sequence to the story?
✔ Does the story move toward a climax?
✔ Has the problem been resolved?

In addition to creating a story that makes sense, students must proofread to insure that the work is both precise and grammatically correct. However, students need a purpose and plan to follow. It may be too general an assignment for students to proofread their work. At first, try limiting the scope of the proofreading, and then expand this list as they become increasingly competent writers.

Using the reproducible found on page 54, have students develop their own individualized proofreading list based on the punctuation and grammatical skills that give them trouble. The list serves as a reminder of errors to look for when students are proofreading. You can also add to the list when reviewing students' work. During the year, the list can evolve with skills added or taken off as needed.

Using SPLOME for Writing

Keep this page in your writing notebook so you'll have it handy when working on writing assignments.

Set goals:
- Identify the type of assignment.
- Identify the purpose of the assignment.
- Know the specific requirements.
- Know how the assignment will be evaluated.

Plan:
- Know the due date.
- Make a schedule.
- Develop a topic by brainstorming ideas or making a concept map.

Link:
- Make connections to the topic: What do you already know? What have you read? How will the information help you in future learning?

Organize:
- Organize the space where you will write.
- Organize the materials you will use.
- Make an outline to help organize your thoughts.

Monitor:
- Reread the assignment. Be sure you are following the guidelines.
- Revise.
- Edit.
- Proofread.

Evaluate:
- Ask: Is the assignment on target?
- Grade your work in your own mind.

Writing a Paragraph

A paragraph is about one topic. The main idea focuses the topic
and gives the paragraph direction. It is developed by the
ideas in the body of the paragraph.

The main idea tells what the paragraph is about. Write the main idea on the lines below.

_____

_____

_____

_____

_____

Sentences found in the body of the paragraph contain information that supports the main
idea. Below, write sentences that contain details, facts, examples, or opinions that support
the main idea.

_____

_____

_____

_____

_____

The final sentence of a paragraph either summarizes or concludes the paragraph, or acts
as a transition, moving the ideas forward to the next paragraph. On the lines below, write
the paragraph's conclusion or transition.

_____

_____

_____

_____

_____

Scholastic Professional Books

Paragraph Checklist

Once you have written a paragraph, reread, edit, and proofread it with the help of this checklist.

1. Paragraph structure

_____ The main idea is clearly stated with supporting details.

_____ It is united.   _____ It is logical.   _____ It is in a meaningful order.

2. Topic sentence

_____ The topic sentence is clear.

_____ The topic sentence is logical.

3. Details

_____ Details are included.

The support sentences

_____ stick to the topic.

_____ elaborate the topic.

_____ develop the topic.

_____ provide examples.

4. Concluding sentence

The concluding sentence

_____ summarizes the paragraph.

_____ moves the reader toward the next paragraph.

_____ answers the question.

5. Sentences

The sentences

_____ vary in length.

_____ vary in types (statements, questions, commands, or exclamations).

6. Proofreading

_____ The spelling is correct.

_____ The punctuation is correct.

_____ The capitalization is correct.

Story Outline

A well-written story includes the following parts.
Use this outline to help you organize your story.

Title:

_____

Characters and Descriptions:

- _____

- _____

- _____

Setting:

- _____

- _____

- _____

Problem:

_____

_____

_____

Plot Sequence:

- _____

- _____

- _____

Solution:

_____

_____

_____

Responding to Books

By keeping a response journal for books you have read, you not only focus on what you read, but also develop useful material for writing book reports and reviews, and even stories of your own. Here are some questions that you might answer in a response journal.

Setting:

- Does the setting seem real?
- Does the author use senses, such as sight and hearing, in the descriptions?
- Would you like to be in a place like that?
- What would it be like to live during the time in which the story takes place?
- How does the setting make you feel?

Characters:

- Do any of the characters remind you of someone you know? What traits do they share?
- How does the author support or justify the characters' actions?
- How would you have reacted to the situations in the story? Is this similar to or different from how the characters reacted?
- What did you particularly like or dislike about one of the characters?
- What are your favorite quotes from the characters?

Plot:

- What problem or problems do the characters face?
- What is the most exciting part of the story?
- Are there surprises? What are they?
- Have you ever had a similar experience?
- Would you change the solution? How?

Author:

- How would you describe the author's style?
- What do you find most effective about the author's writing?

General:

- Why did you enjoy the book?
- Why didn't you like the book?
- How would you change the book?
- If you could give the book a different title, what would it be?

Book Report Form

Use this form to help you remember key information
to include in a book report.

Book Title: _____

Author: _____

Main Idea: _____

Character 1
- Name: _____
- Description: _____
- Purpose: _____

Character 2
- Name: _____
- Description: _____
- Purpose: _____

Character 3
- Name: _____
- Description: _____
- Purpose: _____

Problem: _____

Plot/Sequence of Events:
1. _____
2. _____
3. _____

Solution: _____

Comments, Observations, Questions: _____

Summary: _____
_____

Favorite Quotes

Use this form to keep track of your favorite quotes from the story.
Then, using one of the quotes as a starting point,
write a dialogue you might have with a character.

Book Title: _____

Author: _____

Character	Page	Quote

Planning Calendar

Use this calendar to plan your research report. Write the
name of the month on the line above the calendar and
fill in the dates in the smaller boxes. Fill in the larger boxes with
what you need to do to finish the report on time, and in an orderly, organized way.
Give yourself enough time to finish each task separately.

_____

MONTH

Sunday	Monday	Tuesday	Wednesday	Thursday	Friday	Saturday

D u e   D a t e   /   /

Editing Reminders

Editing is the chance to change and improve your work. Begin to edit your work by asking yourself the questions below. It may be helpful to read your work aloud to a parent or friend.

Read through your written piece.

- Does it make sense?
- Does it follow a well-developed outline?
- Does it have a clear, logical, well-organized thesis statement?
- Does the introductory paragraph set up the topic well?
- Does the piece accomplish what you set out to do?
- Is your intention clear to readers?

Next, reread your piece one paragraph at a time.

- Is the main idea clearly stated?
- Is the main idea supported with enough examples and details?
- Are all the sentences connected to that topic?
- Does the information flow?
- Is there any important information missing that a reader will need in order to understand the topic?
- Is there a comfortable and logical transition from one paragraph to the next?

Finally, reread your piece one sentence at a time.

- Is every sentence a complete sentence—not a run on or fragment?
- Does each sentence relate to the main idea?
- Is there enough variety in the types of sentences you've used?
- Have you chosen your words carefully?
- Have you avoided overused words?
- Have you checked to see that all words are spelled correctly?

Personal Proofreading List

Write down the things that give you trouble when you write.
Then, use your personal proofreading list to help you
check your own work.

Capitals

_____

_____

_____

Punctuation

_____

_____

_____

Grammar

_____

_____

_____

Sentences

_____

_____

_____

Spelling

_____

_____

_____

     Scholastic Professional Books

Math

Oh I knew that—it's the same idea!

The sources of difficulty with math are often found in students' undefined, haphazard approaches. Even when basic knowledge seems sound, students can make wild errors. In some cases it is because they don't know the procedure, and attempt to cleverly construct their own. Take, for instance, Jesse. He knew his basic facts and tested well on timed tests of automaticity, but when he added 47 and 38, he got 22. He had not learned the procedure for two digit addition, so he added all four numbers as if the problem were $4 + 7 + 3 + 8$! Another example is Lisa, who didn't estimate or evaluate her answer and ended up with 2000 when .02 should have been the answer to her problem. She commented, "Oh I knew that—it's the same idea!"

How many times have you heard students say, "It was just carelessness! I knew how to do the problem!" You can help students be certain that they really do know what they think they know, and that they can use their knowledge to get the correct answers.

Basic skills
- To have a good math foundation, students must know basic math facts. To learn facts, many students need direction and clear expectations. A good goal for students is to understand math facts well enough to explain and reteach them to a classmate.

Content knowledge
- Math skills develop along a continuum, and well-integrated prior learning is critical for success in each new stage. In each math sequence, there are basic concepts and calculation skills that students must acquire. These skills are developmental—building from one year to the next. Ensure that students have the essential foundation before you start the year's work.

Language skills
- Math has its own language. The terminology associated with math can be tricky for students, and therefore eludes their mastery. Teach math language directly.

Procedural knowledge

- Step-by-step sequences that students must follow to complete basic mathematical operations require specific instruction. Clearly teach the steps, and then have students talk themselves through the process. Many math procedures, such as double-digit multiplication and long division, subtracting fractions, or solving equations, require the use of procedural knowledge. These mathematical operations are not obvious or logical to all. Problem solving in its simplest terms can also be step-by-step, which helps give form and structure to the process. Innovative problem solving requires, among other things, creativity, flexibility, and persistence. But a structured approach provides the foundation for purposeful, systematic, targeted thinking skills that enable students who are not natural problem solvers to get a good start.

Strategic knowledge

- Good strategies can have a positive effect on students' approach to math and help keep them on task. For example, teach students to talk to themselves as they work through a problem so they mediate impulsiveness and do not skip steps. Teach students to evaluate their answers for logic and consistency.

Using SPLOME for Math

You can use SPLOME to help you organize your approach to teaching math.

Set goals:
- What will students learn?

Plan:
- How will I present the lesson?
- How can I make students want to know this?

Link:
- How does this lesson relate to what students already know?
- How can I identify connecting skills so students know the basic skills essential to the work?

Organize:
- What materials are essential?
- How will I set up math examples?

Monitor:
- Which monitoring systems will I stress?

Evaluate:
- How should students evaluate their work?
- How should I evaluate their work?

Multiplication

Often students jump to the conclusion that if they can't remember one or two of their multiplication tables, they can't remember any of them. Boost their confidence by helping students realize what they do know. Pass out copies of the reproducible on page 58. With a study partner, or even as homework, have them check off the boxes they know. Any boxes left blank will help you both realize where they still need help and what to target.

Word Problems

Accomplished problem solvers develop a "dialogue" with themselves about a word problem. Modeling the procedure will teach students to use strategies such as these and develop this kind of dialogue.

1. What is the question? Can I paraphrase it and identify the problem to be solved?
2. What information do I need to answer the question?
3. Is the information apparent and readily available? If so, can the question be answered in one mathematical step?
4. If the information is not readily available, do I need to complete two steps to arrive at the answer? What do I need to do to complete the first step?
5. Is the answer going to be numerically bigger or smaller than the information given?
6. What do I have to do? If it's larger, do I add or multiply? If it's smaller, do I subtract or divide?
7. Will it be helpful to draw a picture?
8. What other strategies will help me?
9. Does the answer need to be labeled?
10. Does the answer make sense? Can I estimate to find out?

Give students copies of the reproducible on page 59 to use when working on word problems.

Multiplication Table

Check off the product boxes of the multiplication tables you already know. If any boxes have not been checked off, you will know where you need more practice or help from your teacher.

X	1	2	3	4	5	6	7	8	9	10	11	12
1	1	2	3	4	5	6	7	8	9	10	11	12
2	2	4	6	8	10	12	14	16	18	20	22	24
3	3	6	9	12	15	18	21	24	27	30	33	36
4	4	8	12	16	20	24	28	32	36	40	44	48
5	5	10	15	20	25	30	35	40	45	50	55	60
6	6	12	18	24	30	36	42	48	54	60	66	72
7	7	14	21	28	35	42	49	56	63	70	77	84
8	8	16	24	32	40	48	56	64	72	80	88	96
9	9	18	27	36	45	54	63	72	81	90	99	108
10	10	20	30	40	50	60	70	80	90	100	110	120
11	11	22	33	44	55	66	77	88	99	110	121	132
12	12	24	36	48	60	72	84	96	108	120	132	144

Name _____   Date _____

Steps to Solving Word Problems

1. Restate the problem in my
own words.

2. Identify and state what I need
to do to solve the problem.

3. Do I have the information I need?

4. Do I have to derive information?

5. What operation should I use?

6. Do I need more than one step?

7. How should I label the answer?

8. Is the answer larger or smaller
than the numbers in the problem?

9. Does the answer make sense?

Homework

Students, parents, and teachers all anguish over homework. Some students consider homework an infringement on their personal time. Many parents are unsure of their role when it comes to homework, and some teachers are equally foggy about their purpose in assigning it.

Homework is a great medium to teach students how to approach a learning task. However, both students and parents need to know and share in your goals and expectations for homework. By designing clear and meaningful homework assignments, you can avoid vague responses from students and uncertain parents who get an end run from their children.

Begin by developing a "Homework Partnership" so that you, your students, and their parents don't function in isolation—but instead work toward a common goal. Make it clear that each partner has certain responsibilities.

From you, the teacher—assign homework that is:
- ✔ meaningful and relevant
- ✔ appropriate
- ✔ clearly communicated
- ✔ graded, with feedback provided

From students:
- ✔ knowledge of the assignment
- ✔ appropriate prerequisite academic skills
- ✔ homework management techniques
- ✔ sufficient preparation
- ✔ assignments turned in on time

From parents:
- ✔ knowledge of your expectations
- ✔ homework structure and environment conducive to learning at home
- ✔ clear, realistic expectations of their child

Using SPLOME for Homework
Use the SPLOME guidelines as you design homework assignments.

Set goals:
- Let students know why you are giving the assignment.
- Make assignments as interesting as possible.
- Clearly explain what you expect them to learn.
- Think about how you will measure their learning.

Plan:
- Require their use of an assignment book and nightly planning.
- Provide assignments that will require students to complete long-range planning of projects.

Link:
- Provide assignments that connect information.

Organize:
- Help students organize their information by letting them know which materials to take home.
- Provide homework folders.

Monitor:
- Assign tasks that help students monitor their own learning.

Evaluate:
- Check and grade students' work.
- Provide additional feedback when possible.

Help students organize their materials, book bags, and study space. Give them time to select the books and materials they need to complete their work. Provide a checklist for those who are inconsistent. Require homework keepers for students who are apt to lose or misplace materials. If needed, periodically have sorting and clean-up session to help students keep their materials, book-bags and desks organized.

You'll also want to be as clear as possible when letting students know the materials they need for a given assignment, exactly what they need to submit, what to do in case of absence, what assignments should be kept for future use, and where and how students should keep them.

Pass out the reproducible on page 68 for students to keep in their assignment books. Periodically (for instance, once per term) use the reproducibles on pages 70–71 to get an idea of how students currently approach homework.

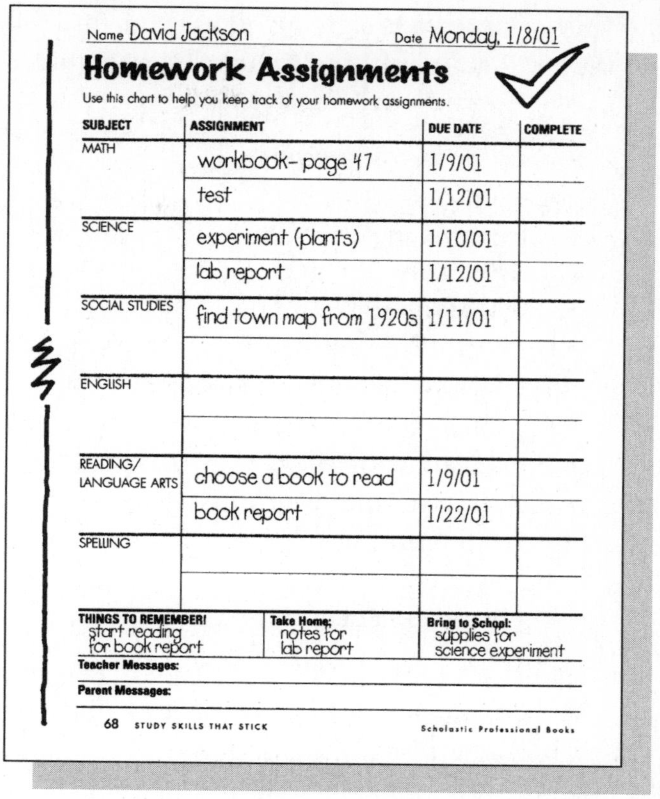
Name David Jackson Date Monday, 1/8/01

Homework Assignments

Use this chart to help you keep track of your homework assignments.

SUBJECT	ASSIGNMENT	DUE DATE	COMPLETE
MATH	workbook- page 47	1/9/01	
	test	1/12/01	
SCIENCE	experiment (plants)	1/10/01	
	lab report	1/12/01	
SOCIAL STUDIES	find town map from 1920s	1/11/01	
ENGLISH			
READING/ LANGUAGE ARTS	choose a book to read	1/9/01	
	book report	1/22/01	
SPELLING			

THINGS TO REMEMBER! start reading for book report | Take Home: notes for lab report | Bring to School: supplies for science experiment

Teacher Messages:

Parent Messages:

68 STUDY SKILLS THAT STICK Scholastic Professional Books

Homework Vision

Answer the following questions to help you assess your vision of homework and what you expect from your students:

In general,

- ✔ who is responsible for the "success" of homework?
- ✔ how do you select homework assignments?
- ✔ what type of homework do you tend to give? Why?
- ✔ do students view homework as punishment?
- ✔ what do parents need to know about homework?
- ✔ do parents know what to expect?

Specifically,

- ✔ what is the purpose of the assignment?
- ✔ what will students learn from the assignment?
- ✔ are your students prepared to do the homework?
- ✔ what skills do students need to bring to the homework process?
- ✔ are students clear about the assignment?

Purpose of Homework

After you have taken some time to assess your own vision and expectations of the homework process, compare it to the following ideas and suggestions concerning the purpose of homework.

Know why you are giving an assignment. Tell students why they are doing it and what they will get out of it. Use this list as a guide.

The purpose of the assignment is to
- preview new material.
- learn facts.
- learn concepts.
- learn vocabulary and terms.
- check for understanding.
- provide a way to see relationships and links between material.
- prepare for class discussion.
- review in-class material.
- organize information.
- identify important information.
- plan to write.
- help study for a test.
- solve a problem.

In addition, explain to students the type of assignment(s) you are giving

The assignment is
- a preview of information to be covered.
- practice and review of information learned.
- a discovery of information.
- an application of existing skills to new situations.
- about problem solving.
- about creativity.

Provide a balance in types of assignments from day-to-day as well as week-to-week. Include assignments that require written work, oral presentation, and group work.

For example, if students have practiced math skills on Monday and they seem to be mastering them, use the same skills for problem solving on Tuesday. Or, have students review their class notes from science and then ask or answer a question based on their notes. This exercise not only has them working with science information, but it also begins to emphasize the importance of note-taking skills.

Tip
Whether you write an assignment on the board, give it orally, or hand out prepared sheets, call on a student to state the main focus of the assignment including when it is due. If you do this consistently, calling on different students each time, students will know they should read the assignment and be prepared to summarize it. It will also be understood that everyone is responsible for knowing what the assignment is.

Homework Assignment Notebook

An assignment notebook is a teaching-learning tool. It is the source and foundation for an organized approach to homework and to learning. The written record helps to prevent the chaos and confusion of unorganized students.

When students use a homework notebook, there are less "I forgot" or "I didn't know" stories. You can teach planning, organizing, and time management through the assignment book while demonstrating the value of knowing what you are doing. Have students use the reproducible sheet (provided on page 68) for keeping track of homework assignments by placing it in the front of their homework notebooks.

A well-kept notebook is
- ✔ a solid record of the course content.
- ✔ an indication of what the teacher thinks is important.
- ✔ a guide for test preparation.
- ✔ an asset to long-range planning.
- ✔ a way to model and guide planning, prioritizing, and time management.

When students use homework notebooks
- set aside time to give the assignments clearly.
- be sure that assignments due later in the week or month are presented in helpful, planned steps.
- have students check to see that they have their assignment book before leaving school.

Time Management

Very often students do not have an accurate sense of how much homework they actually have and complete. Time management is a big deal. Students are likely to say, "I can't do that work. It takes too long," or "I worked for an hour and I couldn't finish it." But how many breaks or other activities might occur in that time? To help students learn a little about time and how they can plan and manage it, have them use a time management sheet. Complete a copy of the reproducible found on page 72 with the class, as an example, before you send it home.

Students also will need help with long range assignments. Here is an example of how they can plan the preparation of a book report over a two-week period.

Assignment: .... Write a book report by developing a new book jacket for a book that is 150 pages in length.

Due date: .... 2 weeks (14 days)

Divide the assignment into daily tasks

Day 1 .... Read the book jacket.

Days 1-10 .... Read 15 pages a day.
.... List and describe the characters as you read.
.... Write the main idea or important changes from each chapter.
.... Jot down ideas for your sales pitch.

Days 8-9 .... Brainstorm about the author.
.... Write a paragraph about the author.

Day 11 .... List points for the summary.
.... Organize a point of view for the sales pitch.

Day 12 .... Write a draft summary with a pitch.

Day 13 .... Edit the rough draft and write the final draft.
.... Use your personal proofreading list.

Day 14 .... Submit the assignment.

Monitoring and Evaluating

Monitoring strategies help students learn from their assignments by involving active reading skills, focused text reading, writing, and rehearsal. You can teach these strategies in class and assign tasks that require the use of monitoring and organizing strategies for homework. For example, instead of telling students to read a chapter, assign preview and prediction tasks. Instead of telling students to write a paper, assign planning and organizing tasks.

Provide assignments that help students monitor their learning and encourage them to learn as they go. Students should keep ongoing records of the work they have done. This will help them realize what they do know and what they still need to know.

As you begin teaching a topic you can identify for students what they will be responsible for learning. You can write a list on the chalkboard for them to copy. Then, remind them to check off the material they master after studying.

You play a critical role in determining the focus, quality, and value of homework. Evaluate students' homework so they know that you consider it important. Let students know how you will keep track of their completed homework assignments and what part homework plays in their final evaluation. How students keep track of their assignments may effect their overall success. Students benefit from knowing exactly which assignments they have completed and which ones still need to be handed in. Try a direct approach such as the letter below.

Dear class,

This is how I will evaluate your homework:

1. I will collect it daily.
2. I will give a P, P-, or P+.
3. Homework must be neat, complete, correct, and have proper headings.
4. You can/cannot correct daily homework and resubmit it.
5. If you are absent, it is your responsibility to get the assignment and make up your homework.

Name _____   Date _____

Homework Assignments

Use this chart to help you keep track of your homework assignments.

SUBJECT	ASSIGNMENT	DUE DATE	COMPLETE
MATH			
SCIENCE			
SOCIAL STUDIES			
ENGLISH			
READING/ LANGUAGE ARTS			
SPELLING			

THINGS TO REMEMBER!	Take Home:	Bring to School:

Teacher Messages:

Parent Messages:

Using SPLOME for Homework

Set goals:
- Know the purpose of the homework assignment.
- Know what is to be learned.
- Know what the teacher expects.
- Know how the assignment will be used.
- Know the grading system.

Plan:
- Use an assignment notebook.
- Set priorities for nightly homework.
- Use a planning calendar to help manage your time.

Link:
- Preview new material.
- Connect previously learned material.
- Establish steps for long-term assignments.

Organize:
- At school,
  - keep a homework notebook, divided by subject.
  - take home material needed for homework.
  - take homework to school and turn it in.
- At home,
  - set up a homework station.
  - set a specified time to do homework.
  - examine homework, prioritize, and allocate time.
- After homework,
  - put your work in a homework folder.
  - pack up your books and homework.

Monitor:
- Be sure that assignments make sense and are correct.
- Be sure you are learning while completing assignments.
- Identify what you learned.
- Identify any material that is confusing and raise questions.
- Ask for help as necessary.

Evaluate:
- Be certain that your work is in acceptable condition.
- Consider the work in relation to your goals.

Keeping Track of Homework ✓

1. Do you use an assignment notebook? _____ Yes _____ No

2. If yes, please explain how you use the assignment book. _____
   _____
   _____

3. If no, please explain how you know what homework has been assigned. _____
   _____
   _____

4. Do you usually know what the teacher expects from you? _____ Yes _____ No

5. How does homework fit into the overall class picture? _____
   _____
   _____

6. Do you know how the homework is graded? _____ Yes _____ No

7. How long does it take you to complete your homework? _____
   _____

8. Do you plan your nightly assignments? _____ Yes _____ No

9. Do you plan long range projects? _____ Yes _____ No

10. Do you plan how to study for tests? _____ Yes _____ No

11. Do you remember to bring books home? _____ Yes _____ No

12. Do you call classmates for assignments? _____ Yes _____ No

13. Where do you do your homework? _____
    _____

14. Do you complete all assignments? _____ Yes _____ No

15. Do you submit all assignments? _____ Yes _____ No

16. Do you know how you will use your homework? _____ Yes _____ No

    If yes, how? _____
    _____

Homework Success

1. In which class do you have the best homework record? _____

   Why? _____

   _____

2. In which class does your homework record need the most improvement? _____

   Why? _____

3. Where do you keep your work after it is completed, but before you hand it in? ____

   _____

4. What do you do with your homework after it has been graded and returned to you? __

   _____

5. What do you do when you have no specific class assignments? _____

   _____

6. Do you review your class notes? _____ Yes _____ No

   If yes, how? _____

7. Do you preview a chapter before you read it? _____ Yes _____ No

8. Do you take notes while you read? _____ Yes _____ No

9. Do you learn from your assignments? _____ Yes _____ No

10. Are you prepared to participate in class discussions? _____ Yes _____ No

11. Do you identify topics that you do not understand? _____ Yes _____ No

12. Do you ask for explanations or clarification? _____ Yes _____ No

    If yes, whom do you ask? _____

13. Do you know when your work is done well? _____ Yes _____ No

14. Do you know when your work needs improvement? _____ Yes _____ No

15. Do you like the opportunity to redo homework? _____ Yes _____ No

16. Please share one of your homework tips. _____

    _____

    _____

    _____

Name _____   Date _____

Time Management

- Write your assignments on the chart.
- Number each assignment according to the order in which you will complete it.
- Estimate the amount of time it will take for you to complete each assignment.
- Write the time you start and the time you finish.
- Figure out the actual total time that it took to complete each assignment.
- Put a check mark in the "Breaks" box each time you take a break. Next to the check write down the number of minutes the break lasted and what you did during that time.
- Put a check mark in the "Asked for Help" box each time you ask for help. Next to the check write down who helped you.

#	Subject/ Assignment	Estimated Time	Start Time	End Time	Total Time	Breaks	Asked for Help

Ask yourself the following questions:

1. How close was my estimate to the actual time it took to complete the assignments?
2. Why was the time similar or different?
3. Can breaks be helpful in completing my homework assignments?
4. Which breaks helped me? Why?
5. Which breaks did not help me? Why?

72 STUDY SKILLS THAT STICK   Scholastic Professional Books

Test Preparation

You've heard it all and then some.

> "You didn't tell us you were giving a test today!"

> "You said the test would be on the Civil War—you didn't mention anything about Abraham Lincoln."

And perhaps the most frustrating response of all:

> "I study, and I think I know the stuff, but when I take the test, all the information seems to fly out of my head."

For many students, tests create crises of one sort or another. You can work to change this by helping students prepare and analyze their test-taking skills.

Begin by taking the approach that tests are not only a means of evaluating progress, but a learning opportunity as well. If you teach a systematic approach to test preparation, you can provide students with a more positive spin on learning. Let students know that

- ✔ tests help focus their learning.
- ✔ tests give them an opportunity to connect information.
- ✔ tests give them an opportunity to show what they know.
- ✔ tests alert them to what they don't know and where they need help.
- ✔ test results show you, as their teacher, that a different type of instruction might work better.

Before a Test

You can help students prepare for tests in a number of ways.

- Announce tests and projects well in advance.
- Carefully specify the topics and materials that you will cover on a test. (For instance, many students don't think that handouts are part of the real assigned material.)
- When you announce a test, provide students with copies of the Test Prep reproducible on page 76.

- Inform students about the test format and type of questions. If students will be taking a test involving reading comprehension, provide them with the reproducible on page 77.
- Be specific about ongoing evaluation. For example:
  - "There will be a spelling test every Friday."
  - "You will have graded in-class writing every Monday."
- Remind students the day before a test or quiz. If you give pop quizzes, remind students of the possibility.
- Tell students how you will evaluate tests and quizzes.
- Provide guidelines for students to use when studying for a test. For example:
  - "Put all your notes together, then review and outline them."
  - "Develop questions that you think might be on the test and share them with the class."
  - "List and define important terms."
- Have students identify and focus on material that has been hard for them to learn or that they think will give them trouble on a test.

During a Test

Even when students know the material, they may find the test event difficult. Provide the reproducible test-taking guidelines (found on page 78) beforehand to make test time manageable.

Tip
Remind students to wait until they are told to start a test. If students feel anxious, suggest they take a deep breath, count to ten, or close their eyes for a moment and think of a beautiful scene.

After a Test

The testing process is not over when a test is done. Students need to know about their test work. They need to consider how well they prepared for the test and how effectively they performed. You can use test results to compare a student's (and your own) expectations to his or her performance. Test results also provide insights into how students can change their preparation and how you can adjust your teaching.

- Review the tests with students so they see the relationship between their work and the expected answers.
- Model good written answers.
- Have students correct tests either in class or at home. Provide feedback by grading or commenting on these corrections.
- Have students complete test analysis questionnaires (pages 79 and 80) with you. Use these as the basis for planning future learning.
- Review test grades to determine if there is pattern of success or failure. If necessary, reteach material where students demonstrate a real lack of understanding.
- Plan mini-lessons on aspects of test-taking that students haven't mastered.

In short, let students know that you want them to succeed and you are ready to help them do so.

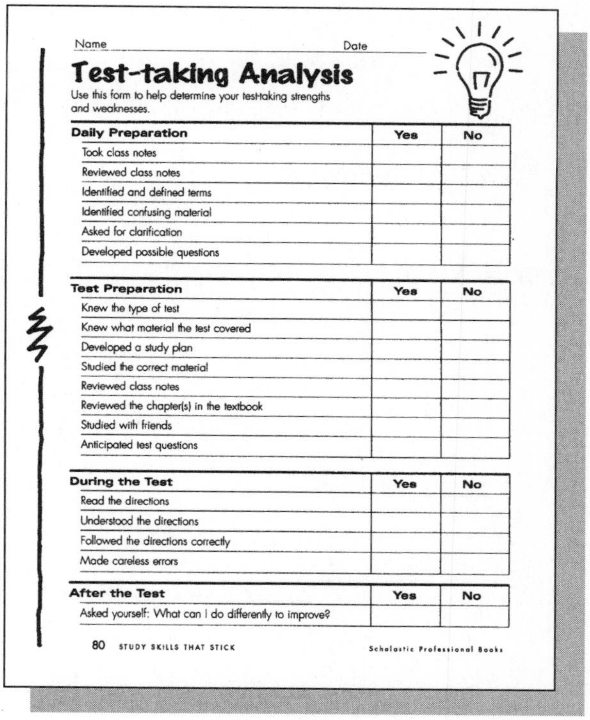

Name Date

Test-taking Analysis

Use this form to help determine your test-taking strengths and weaknesses.

Daily Preparation	Yes	No
Took class notes		
Reviewed class notes		
Identified and defined terms		
Identified confusing material		
Asked for clarification		
Developed possible questions		

Test Preparation	Yes	No
Knew the type of test		
Knew what material the test covered		
Developed a study plan		
Studied the correct material		
Reviewed class notes		
Reviewed the chapter(s) in the textbook		
Studied with friends		
Anticipated test questions		

During the Test	Yes	No
Read the directions		
Understood the directions		
Followed the directions correctly		
Made careless errors		

After the Test	Yes	No
Asked yourself: What can I do differently to improve?		

80 STUDY SKILLS THAT STICK Scholastic Professional Books

Test Prep

Subject: _____

Test date: _____

Test topic: _____

Material covered:

    Chapter(s) _____ Pages _____

Questions to focus on: _____

_____

Check the materials you will use.

_____ class notes   _____ review sheets/handouts from teacher

_____ past quizzes/tests   _____ past homework assignments

_____ worksheets   _____ essays/other written work

Check the test formats you will use.

_____ short answer

     _____ true/false   _____ fill-in blank

     _____ matching   _____ multiple choice

_____ essay

     _____ persuasive   _____ expository

     _____ compare and contrast   _____ descriptive

_____ using graphic material

     _____ charts   _____ graphs

     _____ diagrams   _____ news cartoons

     _____ maps   _____ timelines

Check the study strategies you will use.

_____ paraphrase text   _____ write possible test questions

_____ make an outline   _____ create semantic maps

_____ draw a time line   _____ reread

_____ list and define key terms   _____ other: _____

 Scholastic Professional Books

Test Questions

Many reading tests include the six types of questions listed here.
Learn to identify these types of questions before you attempt to answer them.

1. Main Idea

The main idea is the focus of a passage. Main idea questions ask you to identify the overall topic of a passage. Sometimes these questions ask you to choose or write the best title for a passage.

2. Factual

Factual questions often are about details or examples used to develop the passage's main idea. The answers to factual questions can be found in the passage.

3. Vocabulary

Vocabulary questions seek the definition of a word as it is used in the passage. Often, vocabulary questions can be derived from reading the words, phrases, and sentences near the word.

4. Inferential

Inference questions ask you to use information that is suggested but not directly stated to form an answer. Inference questions often include words such as *imply*, *infer*, and *conclude*.

5. Sequential

These questions usually refer to time order or the order in which something is done. Answer these questions carefully because the events or steps may not appear in sequence in the passage.

6. Author

These questions may ask about the author's point of view, tone, or purpose in writing something. The questions may ask the following: What is the author's opinion? What tone does the author take in writing this passage? Why did the author write this passage?

During a Test

Understand the directions.

- Read them or listen to them carefully.
- Pay close attention to tests with specific answer requirements such as

  filling in circles, underlining, circling, or showing how you arrive at a math solution.
- Underline important words.
- Paraphrase instructions in your head.
- Listen for last-minute instructions.
- Study examples if they are given.
- Scan the test to determine the type of questions asked.
- Ask for the teacher clarification.

Establish a time frame.

- Know what time the test begins and ends.
- Identify how much time is allotted for the whole test and each type of question or section.
- Watch the time as you work.

Use good test sense.

- Move carefully and systematically from one question to the next.
- Don't automatically choose the first answer you think is correct. Read every answer.
- If you are not certain of an answer,
    - eliminate the choices that are obviously wrong to narrow the possibilities.
    - reread the question and select the answer that makes the most sense.
    - if needed, make your best choice.

If you skip a question

- put a check next to it so you can return to it if there is time.
- skip the number on the answer sheet if you are using one.

Sources of Success and Error

Use this questionnaire to help determine why you were successful on a test or why you made certain errors.

Success attributed to:	Yes	No
Preparation		
Appropriate review		
Time used efficiently		
Tried different approach to the work		
Anticipated possible questions		
Read all information for multiple choice questions		
Checked answers		
Worked carefully		

Errors caused by:	Yes	No
Anxiety		
Insufficient information		
Confusing questions		
Misinterpreted questions		
Confusing answers		
Incomplete answers		
Impulsiveness		
Lack of focus		
Lack of self-questioning		
Did not evaluate answers		
Difficulty with a specific type of question		

Name _____   Date _____

Test-taking Analysis

Use this form to help determine your test-taking strengths and weaknesses.

Daily Preparation	Yes	No
Took class notes		
Reviewed class notes		
Identified and defined terms		
Identified confusing material		
Asked for clarification		
Developed possible questions		

Test Preparation	Yes	No
Knew the type of test		
Knew what material the test covered		
Developed a study plan		
Studied the correct material		
Reviewed class notes		
Reviewed the chapter(s) in the textbook		
Studied with friends		
Anticipated test questions		

During the Test	Yes	No
Read the directions		
Understood the directions		
Followed the directions correctly		
Made careless errors		

After the Test	Yes	No
Asked yourself: What can I do differently to improve?		

Scholastic Professional Books